DATE DUE			
M.H.C. DEC 10 '73 LIBRARY			
APR 28 '70 LIBRARY			
GAYLORD			PRINTED IN U.S.A.

Less Time, More Options

Less Time, More Options

EDUCATION BEYOND THE HIGH SCHOOL

A Special Report and Recommendations by
The Carnegie Commission on Higher Education

JANUARY 1971

MCGRAW-HILL BOOK COMPANY
New York   St. Louis   San Francisco   Düsseldorf
London   Sydney   Toronto   Mexico   Panama
Johannesburg   Kuala Lumpur   Montreal
New Delhi   Rio de Janeiro   Singapore

Andrew S. Thomas Memorial Library
MORRIS HARVEY COLLEGE, CHARLESTON, W. VA.

The views and conclusions expressed in this report are solely those of the members of the Carnegie Commission on Higher Education and do not necessarily reflect the views or opinions of the Carnegie Corporation of New York, The Carnegie Foundation for the Advancement of Teaching, or their trustees, officers, directors, or employees.

Copyright © 1971 by The Carnegie Foundation for the Advancement of Teaching. All rights reserved. Printed in the United States of America.

Additional copies of this report may be ordered from McGraw-Hill Book Company, Hightstown, New Jersey 08520. The price is $1.95 a copy.

Foreword

In early 1967, The Carnegie Foundation for the Advancement of Teaching created this Commission to examine and make recommendations regarding the vital issues in higher education in the United States as we approach the year 2000. We selected these major concerns of higher education for study and investigation: structure, function, and governance; innovation and change; demand, resources, costs, and expenditures; and efficiency in use of resources.

Although the final report of the Commission will not be issued until 1972, when all its research projects have been completed, we have decided to issue special reports on certain urgent or particularly basic matters as soon as we have had the opportunity to clarify our views and to develop specific recommendations.

This special report, *Less Time, More Options: Education Beyond the High School,* examines and makes recommendations concerning a topic that is central to every other aspect of higher education —the general flow of students into and through the formal structure of higher education in the United States and the key role played by degrees in this flow. Recommendations are set forth calling for basic changes in the pattern of this flow. Subsequent Commission reports will present a detailed analysis of the impact of these recommendations, if implemented, on the number of students in college at any one time in the future and the amount of resources that will be required to support higher education. These potential impacts will be contrasted with estimates of future numbers of students and resource requirements if current flow patterns are continued unchanged.

The present report proposes increasing the effective options available to students to stop out from college. This is not to suggest that the Commission assumes that the only possible choice is between college courses with curricula as now structured and stopping out. A forthcoming report of the Commission on academic reform will consider ways to make college more valuable to students and ways to combine study and service as an integral part of college experience, thus expanding choices within the higher education system. These proposals may reduce both the desire to stop out and the necessity to stop out for experience.

Two studies sponsored by the Carnegie Commission and published by the McGraw-Hill Book Company were particularly valuable reference sources for this report: *Academic Degree Structures: Innovative Approaches,* by Stephen H. Spurr, and *Colleges of the Forgotten Americans,* by E. Alden Dunham.

Eric Ashby
The Master
Clare College
Cambridge, England

Ralph M. Besse
Chairman of the Board
The Cleveland Electric Illuminating
  Company

Joseph P. Cosand
President
The Junior College District
  of St. Louis

William Friday
President
University of North Carolina

The Honorable Patricia
  Roberts Harris
Partner
Strasser, Spiegelberg, Fried, Frank,
  and Kampelman, Attorneys
Washington, D.C.

David D. Henry
President
University of Illinois

Theodore M. Hesburgh
President
University of Notre Dame

Stanley J. Heywood
President
Eastern Montana College

Carl Kaysen
Director
Institute for Advanced Study
  at Princeton

Kenneth Keniston
Professor of Psychology
Yale University School of Medicine

Katharine E. McBride
President Emeritus
Bryn Mawr College

James A. Perkins
Chairman of the Board
International Council for
  Educational Development

Clifton W. Phalen
Chairman of the Executive
  Committee
Marine Midland Banks, Inc.

Nathan M. Pusey
President
Harvard University

David Riesman
Professor of Social Relations
Harvard University

The Honorable William W. Scranton
Chairman
National Liberty Corporation
President
Penn-Texas

Norton Simon

Kenneth Tollett
Professor of Law
Texas Southern University

Clark Kerr
Chairman

Contents

Foreword, iii

1 Major Themes, 1

2 The Importance of the Degree Structure, 3

3 The Current Degree Structure, 5

4 The New Facts and the New Forces, 7

5 Possibilities for Improvement, 11

6 Recommendations, 13

7 Responsibilities, 25

8 Goals for the Future, 31

Appendix A: Selected Master of Philosophy and Doctor of Arts Programs, 33

Appendix B: Council of Graduate Schools Statement on Doctor of Arts Degree, 35

Appendix C: Sandwich Programs in Great Britain and Cooperative Education Programs in the United States, 39

Appendix D: College-Level Examination Program, 41

Appendix E: Bachelor's Degree in Liberal Studies, University of Oklahoma, 43

Appendix F: Total Registered and Elapsed Time from B.A. to Ph.D. by Field, 45

Table 1: A Generalized Model of Success and Attrition in American Colleges and Universities, 9

Table 2: Proposed Flow of Education Beyond the High School, 19

Table 3: Degree Structures—Current and Proposed, 22

1. Major Themes

1 The length of time spent in undergraduate college education can be reduced roughly by one-fourth without sacrificing educational quality.

2 Young people should also be given more options (a) in lieu of formal college, (b) to defer college attendance, (c) to stop out from college in order to get service and work experience, and (d) to change directions while in college.

3 Opportunities for higher education and the degrees it affords should be available to persons throughout their lifetimes and not just immediately after high school.

4 New degrees, particularly the Master of Philosophy (M.Phil.) and the Doctor of Arts (D.A.), should be greatly extended in their use to meet the needs of students and to fit the requirements of their subsequent employments.

5 There should be four generally accepted degree levels (now many institutions use only two, the B.A. and Ph.D.) to reduce the dropout rate and to create more points for reassessment of his college career by the student and of the student by the campus. These four levels should be: A.A., B.A., M.Phil., and D.A. (and Ph.D.).

6 The emphasis on certification through formal higher education should be reduced. Certificates, where necessary, should be broad, rather than narrow, in their coverage; we now have too many highly specialized degrees—about 1,600 in total.

7   These reforms could result in a reduction of operating expenditures for higher education by 10 to 15 percent a year below levels that would otherwise prevail by 1980, or $3 to $5 billion a year. Construction costs in the 1970s could be reduced by one-third, or a total for the decade of $5 billion.

8   More educational, and thus career, opportunities should be available to all those who wish to study part-time or return to study later in life, particularly women and older persons.

9   Society would gain if work and study were mixed throughout a lifetime, thus reducing the sense of sharply compartmentalized roles of isolated students *v.* workers and of youth *v.* isolated age. The sense of isolation would be reduced if more students were also workers and if more workers could also be students; if the ages mixed on the job and in the classroom in a more normally structured type of community; if all members of the community valued both study and work and had a better chance to understand the flow of life from youth to age. Society would be more integrated across the lines that now separate students and workers, youth and age.

2. The Importance of the Degree Structure

The degree structure, a central aspect of the American higher education system, has major impacts on the lives of millions of young persons and on the use of national resources. It significantly influences:

- The amount of time spent by youths in formal higher education and its pattern of continuity
- How this time is used—on what studies and for what purposes
- The amount of resources needed by institutions of higher education and provided by society
- The job expectations and job performances of graduates
- The opportunities for persons throughout their lives to obtain the further education they may come to desire as their lives unfold

These considerations are of great and rapidly increasing importance as education becomes a more necessary part of more of the total lives of more people and as we move into the "learning society" of the future. The learning process will continue to absorb more and more of the life activities of more and more Americans. Learning opportunities should respond to the new dimensions of the life-and-learning process.

3. The Current Degree Structure

The degree structure of today reflects the development of American society and of its system of higher education from colonial dependency to technological modernity.

First, there was the Bachelor of Arts (B.A.) degree (and later the Bachelor of Science) for the student wanting a general education. In this country the first B.A.'s were conferred by Harvard in 1642. Originally, this degree was designed to give middle-class youth an acquaintance with classical and European culture, and study followed a prescribed classical curriculum. After the Civil War the curriculum began to be modified to permit a choice of electives within a spread across the major streams of thought—humanities, social sciences, physical sciences, biological sciences.

Second, there were developed specialized degrees for the historic professions of medicine, law, theology, and teaching. Columbia introduced a medical doctorate in 1770, William and Mary a law degree in 1793, and Yale a Bachelor of Divinity in 1871; and the University of North Carolina awarded the first Master of Arts based upon advanced study in 1856. These degrees were established to certify the competence of the principal professional persons serving a preindustrial society—the doctor, the lawyer, the minister, and the teacher.

Third, came the Ph.D. degree taken over from the German universities. The first was awarded at Yale in 1861. It was a research degree and still remains so at many universities and for many students, but it has also been used, increasingly, as a general port of entry into college teaching. It was, at first, a two-year degree after the B.A. and then a three-year degree. Since World War II it has come to be for a "course of study of indefinite duration." The

Ph.D. programs were intended to help America catch up with and later to lead the scientific revolution with its implications for material wealth and national power.

Fourth, have come a whole series of occupational degrees, like the M.B.A. for executives, the M.S.W. for social workers, and many others—usually at a level between the B.A. and the Ph.D. These occupational degrees of more recent times have reflected the rise of occupations based on formal instruction to serve an ever more complex technology and economic structure and the greatly expanded welfare services such as health care and social work.

The Master of Arts has achieved importance for teaching in secondary schools and community colleges, and the number of Associate of Arts degrees awarded is increasing greatly as the community college movement expands. Altogether there are now about 1,600 separately named degrees in the United States, most of them found in this fourth category.

Each of these major degree developments can be considered a great success. Classical and European culture was brought to the new society. Adequate, and subsequently superb, practitioners were developed in the historic professions. Research of good, and later spectacular, quality was developed in the new society. A modernized nation came to be served by its technically trained personnel at a high level of effectiveness.

The historic degree structure has served America well. The dominant pattern for large segments of higher education is that already set in 1890—primary emphasis on the four-year B.A. and the six- and then eight- and then ten-year Ph.D. as the degree of greatest prestige. This pattern of emphasis continues to meet the needs of many students, many campuses, and many occupations in 1970.

The times, however, are changing. Relatively fewer students, fewer campuses, and fewer jobs are well served by the historic pattern. A fifth stage in the development of degree arrangements is now desirable.

4. The New Facts and the New Forces

Several new developments of substantial impact are coming to bear on the structure of American higher education.

Many more young people attend college. In 1900, 4 percent of the age group went to college; in 1970, 40 percent go to college; 2 out of 3 in California. They are of many more levels of academic ability and academic preparation than in earlier times, from many more cultural backgrounds, and with more diverse career goals. Some—perhaps as many as 1 in 6—are unwilling "captives" of formal higher education, attending against their will because of the pressures of their parents and the expected requirements of the jobs to which they aspire. Many others attend school more steadily or for longer periods or in programs that do not match their interests than either they wish or society requires.

Much more of education takes place before college, outside of college, and after college than ever before. The schools, including the high schools, have improved their quality since World War II, and they can improve still more—much of the last year of high school, in particular, is wasted for those already admitted to college. The students also come to college with more knowledge due to the influence of the higher levels of education of their parents and to the easy availability of TV, books, and films. Many students are one year farther advanced, academically, than their age group was at the end of World War II. The first year of college is often largely wasted for students with a better general background than that to which the colleges earlier adjusted and for students with clear academic or occupational goals who want to get started toward their careers. College students also have more access than ever before to the world around them through TV, travel, and service opportunities. After college, there is more need for continuing occupational training on the job and through course work and more opportunity than ever before for cultural advancement due to more leisure, higher standards of living, and improved means of communication. College today supplies a smaller proportion of lifetime knowledge. It is *one* of many sources of knowledge and less a rare and one-time opportunity. The approach need not be as it once was: everything now and never again. Formal education at any level is more an important part of education than its totality. Education, in all its myriad forms, surrounds modern man.

Jobs have changed. Rather than long-extended formal education in advance, more jobs require some basic skills and knowledge in advance and then a willingness to keep on learning and opportunities to learn. Some occupations and professions, such as those of engineers, doctors, and lawyers, now require, and will increasingly require, periodic formal updating of knowledge. Also, more people experiment with several occupations during their lifetimes and need more opportunities to learn new skills—the shift of the woman from the home to the labor market in the middle of her life is one important illustration. Life-styles also have changed. More people want more variety in their lives through travel, hobbies, and cultural interests; and they want continuing opportunities to acquire new skills and knowledge. Thus it would seem wise to space formal education over the lifetime, reducing the amount of time spent on it early in life and spending additional time on formal education later in life as desired and as needed.

Young people have changed. They reach physiological and social maturity at an earlier age—perhaps by about one year, and yet more of them are kept longer in the dependent status of student. They are more resistant to the seemingly endless academic "grind" that, for more of them, goes on for more and more years without letup, sitting at their desks as recipients of knowledge but without productive contribution. This takes an internal discipline and a fixed concentration on the necessity of the degree for which they are studying which many of them no longer feel. Many of them would like more options to try alternatives as they select their occupations and their life-styles and more chances to try out their productive skills in real-life situations. Sixteen years of education straight through to a B.A. or 20 to 22 to a Ph.D., which is now standard fare on the way to the two most accepted and well-established degrees, does not suit many of them. Many students would like to have productive experience on their way to the degree and to get into regular productive effort earlier in their lives. Productive effort stands for independent status and a sense of personal worth, and formal education for dependency; and there is a revolt against dependency. Productive effort also stands for reality, and formal education too often stands for an artificial hothouse environment that, in excess, has negative consequences for both students and society.

Six out of every ten students enrolling this fall will fail to get the ultimate degree to which they aspire, an overall drop-out rate from higher education of about 60 percent (see Table 1). Most of the dropouts leave without formal recognition for their efforts, and many must have a sense of disappointment and even resentment.

We have learned some things about the educational process. One is that experience outside the classroom can actually benefit classroom performance and make it more meaningful. The high performance of the returning veterans after World War II and of returning Peace Corps volunteers are illustrations; members of

TABLE 1
A generalized model of success and attrition in American colleges and universities* (by percent of entering students)

	Entering	Terminating before securing degree	Securing degree	Securing degree and terminating
Entering college	100			
Undergraduate attrition		47		
Earning bachelor's			53	
Terminating education				23
Entering graduate school†	30			
Master's attrition		11		
Earning master's			19	
Terminating education				11
Entering doctoral program	8			
Doctor's attrition		4		
Earning doctor's			4	
Terminating education				4
TOTAL		62		38

*Generalized data based upon degree statistics and available attrition studies.
†Includes students entering for first-professional degrees.

both groups have done exceptionally well in their academic work. Maturity of judgment and clarity of goals both gain from nonformal educational experience. A second is that it may be hazardous to have a student caste too separated from the realities of the world at work, too immune to the practicalities of actual accomplishments, too removed from contact with their fellow citizens—a class apart. Students have learned of the extent of this gap as they have worked for Senator McCarthy and against the war in Southeast Asia.

America has been described as a *credential society.* To an extent, this is true of all modern industrial societies. Employers, private and public, want evidence of skills acquired and of ability to accept training and the discipline that goes with it. Employment officers, also, minimize the personal risks they encounter by making reference to prior certification rather than relying only on their own judgment. Employers also want maturity before making a permanent employment commitment, although this can be developed in other ways than through added years in formal education. As a consequence of the insistence on degrees, there are fewer careers open to talent, and the nation suffers from the reduced mobility of persons with talent but without the certification of a degree. We regret this and believe that some steps can be taken to offset this trend.

America, also, despite its great recent progress, still distributes opportunities for higher education inequitably. Degrees are more available to the young than to the middle-aged and the old; to men —at a time they can readily be used—than to women; and to members of the higher than to the lower income groups. The American dream promises greater equality than this, and American reality demands that age be served as well as youth, that women be served equally with men, and that the poor be served as well as the rich.

5. Possibilities for Improvement

We believe that improvements in the approach, content, and structure of higher education can make the post–high school experience more advantageous to many individuals and more useful to society. In a forthcoming Commission report on academic reform we will propose improvements in approach and content. In this report we are proposing modifications in the structure of postsecondary education in these directions:

To shorten the length of time in formal education We are convinced that the time spent on the way to the B.A. can be reduced now by one year for many, and subsequently most, students; time spent on the way to the Ph.D. and to M.D. practice can be reduced by an additional one or two years without sacrificing educational quality.

To provide more options We favor more opportunities in lieu of formal college and more stages at which college-going students can change direction, stop out to obtain a noncollege experience, and drop out with formal recognition for work accomplished.

To make educational opportunities more appropriate to lifetime interests We suggest more chances for reentry by adults into formal higher education, more short-term programs leading to certificates, and, generally, more stress on lifelong learning. We oppose the sharp distinctions now made among full-time students, part-time students, and adult students. Education should become more a part of all of life, not just an isolated part of life. An educational interlude in the middle ranges of life deserves consideration.

To make certain degrees more appropriate to the positions to which they lead We shall make specific suggestions.

To make educational opportunities more available to more people, including women, employed persons, older people, and persons from the lower income levels.

With these goals in mind, we suggest below several changes designed to make postsecondary education more forward looking and more adaptable to individual situations than it now is. The proposed changes are not, of course, equally needed or equally desirable in all situations. But the greater range of options proposed should be available somewhere within the system to persons seeking them.

6. Recommendations

That service and other employment opportunities be created for students between high school and college and at stop-out points in college through national, state, and municipal youth programs, through short-term jobs with private and public employers, and through apprenticeship programs in the student's field of interest; and that students be actively encouraged to participate.

We believe not only that all colleges should encourage prospective and continuing students to obtain service and work experience, but also that some colleges may wish to require it before admission or at some point during matriculation and could, in fact, in appropriate instances, grant credit for it toward completion of degree requirements. The federal, state, and municipal governments can assist in this. We believe that the federal, state, and municipal governments, on a permanent basis, should offer service opportunities to young people. Industry should examine its hiring policies and employment patterns to determine ways in which it can provide short-term jobs for young people who wish work experience before taking further formal education. In a recently published Carnegie Commission study of 1961 college graduates, over three-fifths of those responding felt there should be some stopping out either between high school and college or during college.

That the expansion of postsecondary educational opportunities be encouraged outside the formal college in apprenticeship programs, proprietary schools, in-service training in industry, and in military programs; that appropriate educational credit be given for the training received; and that participants be eligible, where appropriate, for federal and state assistance available to students in formal colleges.

The states would need to accredit such programs and should actively plan for them as part of their provision for postsecondary education.

<u>That employers, both private and public, hire and promote on the basis of talent alone as well as on prior certification.</u>

This will require better tests of talent, more exercise of individual judgment by employers and their representatives, more training opportunities on the job, and more concern for ladders to rise and less with ceilings based on prior certification. The best test is performance on the job. The Educational Testing Service (ETS) and the American College Testing Program (ACT) have had great experience with testing and might turn more of their attention to achievement testing as the basis for certificates that will take the place of degrees. Degrees might also be given as a result of these tests by ETS and ACT independently or with a recognized college or university. But, essentially, employers should do more of their own screening for talent and rely less on the instrumentalities of the college, which are designed primarily for other purposes. Greater reliance by employers on tests developed to screen applicants for positions would be vastly less costly to society than using the B.A. degree to screen. Employers and educational leaders should develop informational programs to make certain that such new policies are generally known and particularly that educational advisers and placement officers are aware of the new practices once adopted.

<u>That professions, wherever possible, create alternate routes of entry other than full-time college attendance, and reduce the number of narrow, one-level professions which do not afford opportunities for advancement.</u>

We believe that more careers should be opened up to demonstrated talent, regardless of formal degrees, that nurses should be able to become medical assistants, that technicians should be able to become engineers. Testing procedures will need to be greatly improved to ensure that advancement on the basis of experience meets all the essential requirements of advancement on the basis of degrees. We are particularly concerned with the growth of horizontal craftlike professions in the health services that impede vertical mobility.

<u>That a degree (or other form of credit) be made available to students at least every two years in their careers (and in some cases every year).</u>

Under this policy, students would be given more points at which to reassess their direction, stop out for work experience, or stop with credit. We now have essentially a two-level structure (B.A. and Ph.D.). We suggest a four-level structure (A.A., B.A., M.Phil., D.A. or Ph.D.). Students would be given two-year planning modules that would give them more flexibility than the basically four-year modules now offered on the way to the B.A. and Ph.D.

Not only should students be encouraged to reassess their plans every two years, but the institution should also reassess each student. We believe, in particular, that students should not be encouraged to proceed past the A.A. degree level (lower division) unless and until there is evidence that they have a clear commitment to academic and/or occupational interest requiring additional college training. The college should not help to prolong indefinitely an aimless search for and experimentation with various life-styles and an amateurish sampling of swiftly passing interests; that search seldom benefits either the student or the college. For students who have not made a commitment to college work by the end of the lower division, there are other places where they can explore their potential interests and make up their minds.

We believe, additionally, that there should be the most careful review of a student before allowing him or her to proceed past the M.Phil. level into doctoral study. There is now too seldom a careful check made at this point. The most stringent entrance requirements of all should be set up at this port of entry. Students advanced to candidacy for the Ph.D. should be selected solely on the basis of their research promise.

One way to encourage reassessment of students is to require an affirmative action by the student to apply for the next degree level and an affirmative action by the college to accept him or her. This would reduce the drifting into subsequent stages that now takes place.

<u>That the time to get a degree be shortened by one year to the B.A. and by one or two more years to the Ph.D. and to M.D. practice.</u>

High schools can be accredited by state university systems and by consortia of private colleges to give the equivalent of the first year of work in college. Gradually this could be expanded to cover all, or nearly all, high schools. Fifty thousand high school students are now given credit each year for advanced standing in college. This should quickly be expanded to at least 500,000. Summer-term study can be made available in college for those who do not go to accredited high schools or who have not completed a year of college-level work in accredited high schools. The first year in college can also be made more challenging and useful. Thus the lower division in college could soon become a one-year program except for those needing remedial work. The additional one or two years saved on the way to the Ph.D. and to M.D. practice can be offset by the constant opportunities for additional acquisition of knowledge during careers. The time suggested to be spent in training is quite sufficient to obtain assurance of innate ability and an understanding of basic principles.

That certain new degrees be widely accepted:

The Master of Philosophy Now in effect at the University of Toronto, it calls for two years after the B.A. (see Appendix A). It is useful for persons intending to teach in high schools, community colleges, and in the lower division in colleges. Generally, we favor more such degrees calling for two years of study after the B.A., as does the M.B.A. For example, we favor an M.H.B. (Master in Human Biology), which would equip a person either to be a physician's assistant, or to teach at an appropriate level, or to go on to an M.D. or Ph.D. The two-year advanced master's degree would serve occupations which require more formal training than the one-year M.A. now provides.

The Doctor of Arts Now in effect at Carnegie-Mellon and the University of Washington, it is being offered, developed, or taken under consideration by at least 75 other institutions (see Appendix A). The Ph.D. began as a research degree with the original dissertation at its core. It is a highly respected degree useful for advanced research work and for training students to undertake research. It is less useful for persons who will teach but neither do research nor train research personnel. In fact, for such people it may not only give them a narrower training than their teaching merits but also create pressures both on them to undertake research that does not interest them and on the institutions where they are employed to provide them with reduced teaching loads and facilities for their research.

We favor a Doctor of Arts degree for the nonresearch teacher. (See Appendix B for a statement of the Council of Graduate Schools on the Doctor of Arts degree.) It would take the same length of standard time after the B.A. degree (four years) as the Ph.D. Instead of the dissertation required for a Ph.D., there would be a requirement for some independent piece of work showing understanding of the chosen field of study and ability to present lucidly a complex body of knowledge. The Doctor of Arts degree would also call for (a) a broader field of basic knowledge than the more specialized Ph.D. degree and (b) an opportunity to study and practice pedagogic technique. The D.A. program, as we propose it, would not be a Ph.D. program without the dissertation but would be a specially designed course that would lead to the standard degree for college teachers. The Ph.D. should be reserved for those who clearly intend to engage in original research in their lifetime careers. Salary levels and promotional opportunities should be the same for college teachers whether they have the D.A. or the Ph.D.

We consider it of great importance to reduce the impact of specialization and research on the entirety of higher education. The Ph.D. now has a headlock on much of higher education. The greatest rewards are given to those who are highly specialized in their interests and undertake research, sometimes almost regardless of its importance and their own interest in it. The curriculum nearly all along the line is geared to the interests of the specialized instructor and to training the student for specialization. The requirement of the dissertation orients the student toward his research specialization rather than toward the instruction of students; it sometimes results in a "trained incapacity" to relate to students by both the selection process it sets in motion and the standards of performance it imparts. We now select and train a student to do research; then employ him to teach; and then promote him on the basis of his research. This both confuses him and subverts the teaching process.

We believe it will take a degree with a new name and a new program to declare that teaching is also important and will be equally rewarded and that the narrower and narrower specialization of the past century shall not dominate so much of higher education. The Ph.D. has been a most useful degree. It should be continued as the appropriate degree for those who will undertake original research and train others to do so. But it should be a specialized degree for research personnel, for those who plan to pursue lifelong careers in scholarly investigation. The standard liberal arts advanced degree should be the Doctor of Arts. It should be the degree preferred by colleges for those who are engaged to teach at all levels, with the exception of those who teach specialized research methods.

Development of the Doctor of Arts degree will make the preparation of teachers, as teachers, the concern of all departments and not just the school of education. The rapid growth of community colleges and comprehensive colleges will create a ready demand for persons with the degree. But the basic objective of the Doctor of Arts is not to get more teachers but to get teachers who are better prepared and better oriented. The Doctor of Arts degree will also be appropriate for many positions in government, industry, and academic administration.

The Ph.D. should be available subsequently, on application, to holders of a Master of Philosophy or a Doctor of Arts who can show, through minimum course work or through proficiency certificates or examination, the necessary background, and who also publish an important work of original research or who present a satisfactory dissertation. The competitive test of important research published will often be better proof of ability than an internally evaluated dissertation. Published research would become the functional equivalent of a dissertation. The Ph.D. should also be given to current students for a dissertation satisfactorily completed without the necessity of also fulfilling residence requirements. As a research degree, highly competent research should be its primary requirement, whether performed on campus or off, and the additional background requirements, if any, to be met by holders of the M.Phil. or D.A. should be kept to a minimum and should be determined after individual evaluation of each candidate's total educational and professional experience.

In much the same way that the D.A. is designed for those going into college teaching, a greater use should be made of professional doctorates for clinical practice in psychology, social work, and other fields in which the emphasis is less on research and more on practice.

The proposed flow of education beyond high school based on the above recommendations is set forth in Table 2.

TABLE 2
Proposed flow of education beyond the high school (highly simplified):

1. High school graduation	Enter employment
	Stop out for work or service experience
	Enter college
2. After A.A. degree	Enter employment
	Stop out for work or service experience
	Continue in college
3. After B.A. degree	Enter employment
	Stop out for work or service experience
	Continue in college
4. After M.Phil. degree	Enter employment
	Continue in college
	Receive Ph.D. for published research and completion of any further subject matter requirements deemed necessary for the particular applicant
5. After D.A. degree	Enter employment
	Receive Ph.D. for published research
6. From employment	Receive certification of competence without degree
	Take achievement test for degree
	Reenter college at any time

<u>That opportunities be created for persons to reenter higher education throughout their active careers in regular daytime classes, nighttime classes, summer courses, and special short-term programs, with degrees and certificates available as appropriate.</u>

Higher education is now prejudiced against older students. They should be welcomed instead. Too often they are looked upon as inferior. Yet older students will help end the *in loco parentis* atmosphere of many campuses, add maturity to discussions, and make a more balanced community out of the college.

<u>That opportunities be expanded for students to alternate employment and study, such as the "sandwich" programs in Great Britain and the programs at some American colleges.</u>

Programs at American colleges that combine work experience and formal study are increasing in number and should be encouraged. (See Appendix C.)

<u>That alternative avenues by which students can earn degrees or complete a major portion of their work for a degree be expanded to increase accessibility of higher education for those to whom it is now unavailable because of work schedules, geographic location, or responsibilities in the home.</u>

Recent developments in the United States and in other nations point to increased flexibility in the routes open to persons seeking college degrees:

- The College Level Examination Program makes it possible to obtain college credit for independent study. (See Appendix D.)
- TV and radio college-level courses are recognized by some institutions.
- The mailed syllabus, radio course, local tutorials, and institutional examination form the core of instruction at Britain's new "Open University."
- Independent study, sometimes in combination with tutorials, followed by comprehensive examinations, has long been used by the University of London in its external degree program.

(See Appendix E for descriptions of examples of programs in the United States now in existence which utilize these approaches.)

The future holds the possibility for even greater flexibility in the routes by which persons may obtain degrees:

- Video cassettes and computer-assisted instruction can turn the home into a classroom. In Japan, the Ministry of Education intends to establish an "open university" by 1972 relying heavily on video cassettes that would be available on a rental basis.
- Expansion of college-level examination programs and greater use of off-campus instructional programs may eventually make it possible to earn degrees without any college residence.

<u>That all persons, after high school graduation, have two years of postsecondary education placed "in the bank" for them to be withdrawn at any time in their lives when it best suits them.</u>

This would reduce the pressure to enter college directly out of high school or forgo the opportunity forever. This can be accomplished by (a) providing no- or low-tuition community colleges within commuting distance of nearly all Americans, as we have recommended elsewhere, or (b) by adding to social security a program for "educational security" to be paid through payroll taxes on employers and employees, with the benefits to be available on application after a period of sustained employment, or (c) by making grants, work-study opportunities, and loans available at any time during life, or (d) by providing through employers and unions the opportunity for educational leaves, or (e) by providing educational grants to persons following military and other service activity; or by some combination or combinations of the above programs.

We plan in subsequent reports to set forth in detail our proposals for national, state, and municipal youth programs, for noncollege postsecondary education, for careers open to talent, for "open universities," and for "two-years in the bank."

The degree structure, as we see it, would be as follows (see Table 3):

Associate in Arts awarded after successful completion of a 2-year course of study (with a 1- or a 1½-year option or both available for those with advanced credit from high school) and, as quickly as further acceleration permits, after a 1- or a 1½-year program (with a 2-year option). It would be a terminal degree for (a) those completing certain occupational requirements and (b) those completing their general educational requirements, and as an intermediate degree for those who plan to continue with academic study either directly or after a stop out. This degree should be given full credit by employers in hiring and by institutions of higher education in accepting transfers. For increasing numbers of students it should become the standard degree to which they aspire after they leave high school—but with the expectation that they may and often will return to college later in life.

Bachelor of Arts (or Science) awarded after successful completion of a four-year course of study (with a three-year option immediately available) and as quickly as possible after a three-year course of study (with a four-year option). The British B.A. is now given after three years, except at Keele, with the possibility of a two-year option under consideration.

TABLE 3 *Degree structures—current and proposed*

Current		Proposed	
Years	Degree	Years	Degree
2	Associate in Arts (community colleges only)	2 (1 or 1½)* Later: 1 or 1½ (2)	Associate in Arts (available in all colleges)
4	Bachelor of Arts	4 (3) Later: 3 (4)	Bachelor of Arts
5	Master of Arts	5 (4) Later: 4 (5)	Master of Arts
		6 (5) Later: 5 (6)	Master of Philosophy
8–10 or more†	Ph.D.	8 (7) Later: 7 (8)	Doctor of Arts and Ph.D. *(as specialist degree)*
8	M.D.	7 (6) Later: 6 (7)	M.D.
12	Completion of residency for Medical Doctors	10 (9) Later: 9 (10)	Completion of residency
Short-term	Certificate (community colleges only)	Short-term	Certificate (available in all colleges)

*Figures in parentheses show options to be available—thus "3 (4)" means a normal three-year degree with a four-year option.

†Averages of total *elapsed* years from B.A. degree to Ph.D. are 5 to 15 years, or 9 to 19 years after the high school degree. See Appendix F for registered and elapsed time to the Ph.D. degree.

Master of Arts (or Science) awarded after an additional one-year course of study. It is useful, particularly, for schoolteachers seeking their credentials.

Master of Philosophy (and other similar degrees) awarded after a two-year course of study following the B.A. degree.

Doctor of Arts awarded after a four-year course of study following the B.A. degree.

Doctor of Philosophy awarded after a four-year course of study following the B.A. degree.

Doctor of Medicine awarded after a three-year course of study following the B.A. degree and supplemented by a three-year period, under supervision, as a "house officer," prior to independent practice.

Certificates awarded for shorter courses and specialized courses at any level.

This is a simplified view of the degree structure because there are many additional specialized degrees not noted here, but we would apply the same principles to them as we have to those above. We also suggest that the 1,600 current degrees be reduced to 160 at the most. We believe that the process of reduction would decrease the now increasing emphasis on narrow certification and would lead to a better preparation for work and life. We favor 160 degrees at four fully accepted levels rather than 1,600 at two fully accepted levels. This would provide twice as many points for reassessment by students and of students by the campus, but much fewer narrow channels for students to follow. We recommend that the Council for Graduate Schools consider guidelines for these two developments.

The reforms proposed in this report are primarily motivated by educational policy concerns. We believe, however, that our proposed reforms will result in savings to both the individual and the institution. By all odds, the most important element is the saving in the time of students and the more effective utilization over a person's total life of the time he devotes to education. If the amount of time spent on the way to the B.A. and the Ph.D. and to M.D. practice were reduced by about one-fourth, as we are suggesting, this would also lead to savings in institutional operating costs. Additionally, we suggest that some young persons either not go to college at all or stop at an earlier degree than they now aim for. These impacts would be offset by a reduced drop-out rate as students stayed through the shorter period required to obtain each degree, and, in the longer run, more people would be returning to college. In all, we think that it is realistic to estimate a savings of 10 to 15 percent in institutional operating expenditures by 1980, or $3 to $5 billion a year. This would be offset, in part, by the costs of national and state youth corps programs, which we have recommended above, and perhaps also by the cost of financial aid to older persons who return for periods of formal education.

The savings on capital expenditures would be more dramatic. These recommendations could reduce enrollments in 1980 by about 1 million. Present estimates are for an increase of 3 million more students by 1980, in addition to the more than 6 million now. Even if certain of our recommendations reduced attrition and drew more older people into higher education, it still seems reasonable to assume that the needed new places would be cut by about one-third—to 2 million, and this would result in a total savings of $5 billion on construction during the 1970s.

The federal and state governments are in a period of financial stringency. Many colleges and universities appear now to be in financial difficulties, and many others will face such difficulties in the very near future. Savings of these amounts in the process of improving the structure of higher education should, thus, appear attractive to many decision-making bodies. And many students are impatient with the duration of their formal education.

We should overinvest neither the time of students nor the resources of society in higher education.

7. Responsibilities

The federal government can assist these developments by:

- Assisting the spread of community colleges across the 50 states
- Giving support to students in all postsecondary education, as it did after World War II in the GI Bill of Rights, and not just to those in formal colleges
- Encouraging programs for reducing the length of time in formal higher education through grants from the proposed National Foundation for Higher Education
- Supporting the Doctor of Arts degree financially as it does now the Doctor of Philosophy degree
- Supplying as much money for a three-year M.D. program as for a four-year program
- Creating "youth service" programs on a substantial scale
- Providing better labor market information to students as they periodically reassess their careers
- Encouraging experiments with "open universities" through the proposed National Foundation for Higher Education
- Studying the possibility of an "educational security" program within Social Security

The state governments can assist by:

- Developing community colleges
- Making all postsecondary education, and not just formal colleges, part of their planning process
- Encouraging publicly supported and publicly assisted colleges to reduce the time spent toward a B.A. and a Ph.D.

- Strengthening high schools to take over the work now given in the first year of college
- Supporting the Doctor of Arts degree in publicly supported and publicly assisted universities
- Supplying as much money for a three-year M.D. program as for a four-year program
- Creating "youth service" programs
- Giving colleges and universities extra financial support for older students since special adjustments will often need to be made for them in admissions, in provision of nighttime courses, and in other ways

Foundations can assist by:

- Supporting experimental programs in several of these areas, particularly the Doctor of Arts and testing

Employers and unions can assist by:

- Creating short-term and apprenticeship programs for students during stop-out periods
- Selecting and promoting employees more on the basis of talent and less on prior certification
- Establishing in-service and out-service training programs
- Giving educational leaves
- Encouraging and assisting "sandwich programs" (alternate periods of work and study)

Parents can assist by:

- Encouraging their children to use the final year of high school to obtain advanced standing in college
- Not pressing their children too hard to enter higher education if they have no clear academic interests or occupational objectives, or to undertake higher education too soon after high school, or to stay with it too steadily, or to proceed with higher education beyond their own academic and occupational interests

Students can assist by:

- Making better use of the fourth year in high school
- Exploring employment and service opportunities before entering college and at stop-out points in college
- Determining their academic and occupational interests before proceeding past lower-division work
- Welcoming adult students into what is now the "youth culture" of college

Professional associations can assist by:

- Creating, to the extent possible, alternative methods of entry aside from formal education
- Making each profession sufficiently broad so that it may include a "ladder" of positions, not one "layer" only—again to the extent possible

High schools can assist by:

- Preparing to take over work now given in the first year of college

  This will require a transformation of the fourth year of high school in content and method to make it more interesting and more rewarding.

Colleges and universities can assist by:

- Individually, or through consortia, working with and accrediting high schools to give work now given in the first year of college
- Admitting students with advanced standing, looking to the time when the standard term of a B.A. degree will be three years
- Admitting students, so that they will have a sense of security, but allowing them to postpone actual enrollment for a reasonable period—perhaps three years
- Transforming the first year of college to reflect the enhanced competence of high school graduates and the actual needs of individual students—the opportunities for academic reform are substantial in the process of making the adjustments we suggest

- Encouraging students to have work or service experience before entering college, to stop out while in college to obtain it, or both
- Recognizing more fully and extending the use of the Associate of Arts degree
- Accepting, and even preferring, the Master of Philosophy and Doctor of Arts degrees for their faculty members and paying and promoting persons with these degrees on a basis equal to that of those who have the Ph.D.
- Providing opportunities for and accepting students of all ages
- Introducing "sandwich" courses for students with regular employment
- Providing better counseling, guidance, and advice to students as they periodically reassess their careers

Universities can assist by:

- Offering the Master of Philosophy and Doctor of Arts degrees and shifting resources to them from the Ph.D. programs
- Shortening the time on the way to the Ph.D. and the M.D. — a way to do this is to set a limit on the number of years a student can be counted by a department for purposes of fiscal support
- Providing for a Ph.D. degree after the M.Phil. or D.A. on the basis of superior research publication without additional residence requirements

The Council of Graduate Schools can assist by:

- Considering guidelines for new graduate degree structures
- Encouraging experimentation with tests to determine competence as an alternative to formal degrees or as a method of securing formal degrees

Accrediting agencies can assist by:

- Recognizing that the reforms proposed may require new and different standards for accreditation of institutions and programs

Testing agencies can assist by:

- Creating tests as a basis for college credit in lieu of formal course work
- Creating tests to aid employers in judging competence without a requirement of college credit

8. Goals for the Future

BY 1980:

- Community colleges spread across the nation.
- Associate in Arts degrees generally available in all colleges.
- "Youth service" programs widely established.
- State planning includes all postsecondary education.
- Federal support to students includes all postsecondary education.
- The average length of time to a B.A. degree shortened initially to $3\frac{1}{2}$ years, on the average, and then to 3 years.
- The average length of time to a Ph.D. degree shortened to 4 years after the B.A.
- The standard length of time to an M.D. degree shortened to 3 years and of a residency to 3 years.
- The Master of Philosophy and Doctor of Arts degrees generally accepted.
- "Sandwich" programs introduced at more institutions.
- Experiments undertaken with "open universities."
- An "educational security" program in advanced planning stages.
- Tests fully developed and accepted in lieu of formal course work and in lieu of college credit.

BY 2000:

- "Open universities" well established.
- An "educational security" program in full operation.

These reforms, if accomplished, would be the most significant undertaken since the modern system of higher education emerged from the classical college beginning a century ago. Formal higher education would absorb less of the time of students and less of the resources of society, and it would, at the same time, serve better both the interests of the students and the needs of society. We need more paths and more rates of progress to individual self-fulfillment and to service to society.

Appendix A: Selected Master of Philosophy and Doctor of Arts Programs

MASTER OF PHILOSOPHY, UNIVERSITY OF TORONTO

Admission open to students with the equivalent of I or II class honors in final year of an honor course for a bachelor's degree.

Completion of a two-year program of advanced study and scholarship approved by the department and the degree committee of the appropriate division.

Adequate reading knowledge of one language other than English.

In addition to the prescribed program of course and seminar work, the candidate shall, under a director designated by the department, pursue independent scholarship culminating in a major essay or research paper.

A final examination including the Phil.M. essay or research paper with at least a part of the examination oral.

Appraisal of the essay or research paper and that part of the examination related to it by a representative of the degree committee. (SOURCE: University of Toronto, *School of Graduate Studies Calendar,* 1969–70, pp. 29, 30.)

The [Phil.M.] program was initiated in 1964–65 with 29 students enrolled primarily in the language departments. In the following year, 23 new candidates were enrolled and by autumn of 1966, eight candidates had received the new degree. Of the first group of degree recipients, most were employed immediately by Canadian universities and colleges (including the University of Toronto itself) while two decided to proceed on to the Ph.D. A Phil. M. graduate who proceeds on to the Ph.D. is not subject to additional residence requirements, although he may require more time to complete his studies than a student who has concentrated solely on obtaining the Ph.D.

The Toronto Master of Philosophy, therefore, is a two-year upgraded master's program offering a more general programming of liberal arts courses to a separately admitted group of students. It differs from the Candidate of Philosophy approach in the United States in that the C.Phil.

normally requires three rather than two years, is offered to students who are admitted as regular Ph.D. applicants, and represents the completion of the general studies phase of the doctorate rather than of a separate core program of studies. (SOURCE: Stephen H. Spurr, *Academic Degree Structures: Innovative Approaches,* McGraw-Hill Book Company, New York, 1970, p. 73.)

DOCTOR OF ARTS (MATHE-MATICS)

Carnegie-Mellon, Carnegie Institute of Technology

In addition to the general requirements for the doctorate, candidates for either the Doctor of Philosophy or the Doctor of Arts in Mathematics must complete such courses and engage in such duties as may be required by the department. All doctoral candidates must teach during at least one year of their tenure, and the D.A. candidate has an additional commitment to curriculum planning in the department. While there are no specific course or unit requirements, few students would be considered prepared for either the Ph.D. research thesis or the D.A. expository thesis with less than 15 one-semester graduate courses in Mathematics. A reading knowledge of two languages from among French, German and Russian is required for the Ph.D. degree. The D.A. candidate will almost certainly find it necessary to do some reading in foreign languages, but there is no formal language requirement for the degree. (SOURCE: *Carnegie-Mellon Graduate Studies, Carnegie Institute of Technology,* 1968–70, p. 44.)

DOCTOR OF ARTS (GERMAN)

Excerpt from the proposal for a Doctor of Arts program in German at the University of Washington

In contrast to the traditional Ph.D. curriculum, the D.A. program does not emphasize specialization in limited fields, but rather the broad knowledge of German civilization in its relevant aspects. Furthermore, it familiarizes the student with pertinent problems in Education, Psychology, Anthropology and Philosophy. Thus, it may be considered an interdepartmental program which allows the student to take a limited number of credits (18 credits out of 54 post M.A. credits) in other departments which have a significant impact on the student's own area of interest.

. . . The D.A. dissertations will be limited in scope and they will reflect the students' combined interests in the fields of literature, culture and pedagogy.

. . . It is understood that we will stay in contact with the D.A.'s who are starting out on their teaching careers. We feel that our academic reputation is at stake, and therefore, their success as college teachers is of vital concern to us. One of the duties of our D.A. supervisors and coordinators will be to give further advice and assistance to D.A.'s who hold their first teaching assignments. On the other hand, the experience and retrospective comments of our D.A.'s will be a further source of information in the interest of program improvement.

Appendix B: Council of Graduate Schools Statement on Doctor of Arts Degree

On December 6, 1968, the Council of Graduate Schools endorsed "in principle" the following statement on the Doctor of Arts degree prepared by the council's Committee on the Preparation of College Teachers:

THE DOCTOR OF ARTS DEGREE

The Executive Committee of the Council of Graduate Schools and the Council have in principle recommended the establishment of graduate programs leading to the degree Doctor of Arts to prepare graduate students for a lifetime of effective teaching at the college level.

The Doctor of Arts program should be of such rigor that the degree will take its place among other respected doctoral degrees such as the Doctor of Philosophy, Doctor of Education, Doctor of Medicine, Juris Doctor, and others.

The new title is proposed in the belief that the Ph.D. degree has traditionally so emphasized research that it may be counter-productive in that many graduate students are trained along lines other than those which they will actually follow in their careers as college teachers. The Ph.D. is and should be the highest research degree; many of its recipients do in fact become excellent teaching scholars. However, others are led into expectations that will not in fact be realized, and, as a result, their level of discontent and dissatisfaction may be magnified. Relevance is achieved best if the degree structure is appropriate to the career aims and possibilities of the students as well as to the primary role of most as teaching scholars.

For many doctoral students, a program emphasizing broad subject matter competence and teaching skills and the development of synthesizing and disseminating abilities will be most appropriate. The title Doctor of Arts should connote this great emphasis on preparation of college teaching.

The orientation and preparation inherent in the Doctor of Arts degree have advantages beyond those for the teaching faculty who will find a greater continuity between their training and their actual careers. Colleges will be placed under less pressure to create research facilities if research accomplishment is no longer held up as the one single mark of success of undergraduate faculties. The present influence of research specialization on the undergraduate curriculum would also be reduced, and many students will welcome a broader orientation in curricular offerings. Much of the undergraduate curriculum today is oriented toward the research interest of the faculty members or toward the two percent of the students who will eventually seek the Ph.D. degree. We should now recognize that the great growth in enrollments and thus in teaching positions in the future will be in the community colleges, the comprehensive regional colleges, and in the university colleges—not in the research positions available in the universities or elsewhere.

The Committee recognizes that it is neither feasible nor desirable to separate sharply a university professor's teaching and research functions. Research activity is in many cases an essential element of a professor's teaching effectiveness and all graduate study must include research components. But the importance of research as a component of college teaching is considerably less for those not teaching at the Ph.D. level, and this group constitutes the majority of teachers in higher education. The necessity for research competence and activities at these other levels varies at least quantitatively and in emphasis, depending upon the subject being taught. For most college faculty it seems clear that the research competence required for the great majority of college teachers can be obtained through the proposed Doctor of Arts program.

General Characteristics

The Degree Doctor of Arts identifies a person with at least three years of graduate study and is designed to prepare students for careers as college teachers.

The program leading to the Doctor of Arts degree will parallel other doctoral programs but will be oriented toward developing teaching competence in a broad subject matter area. In contrast, the Doctor of Philosophy program is designed to prepare a graduate student for a lifetime of creative activity and research, although it will often be in association with a career in teaching at a university or college. The degree Doctor of Education (Ed.D.) should mark a professionally oriented program at the doctoral level in the field of education.

The Doctor of Arts program should be offered only by institutions with faculty, facilities, and equipment adequate to provide for the offering of these practice-oriented Doctor of Arts programs; they must be comparable in quality, although different in character, to accepted research-oriented Ph.D. programs.

Admission, retention, and degree standards for a Doctor of Arts program should be as rigorous as those prevailing for a Ph.D. program and should be under the control of the graduate faculty of the subject-matter field. Under no circumstances should the Doctor of Arts be utilized as a consolation prize or second class, attenuated Ph.D. While program requirements will inevitably differ because of different objectives, requirements for the

Doctor of Arts should be no less demanding. If it is awarded at the completion of a program equal in quality and rigor to the Ph.D., its recipients should be employed in their areas of competence on a comparable basis to those holding the Ph.D. The standards and reputation of the graduate school awarding the degree are the significant determinants.

Special Characteristics

To insure adequate preparation of college teachers, the Doctor of Arts program should provide for the following:

First, the formal course work in the Doctor of Arts program will deal preponderantly with the subject matter to be taught by the prospective teacher. Course selection will typically be broader within a particular discipline than for the Ph.D. and may also bridge several related disciplines. The individual courses in the Doctor of Arts program will be conducted at the same high level as Ph.D. courses and where the two programs exist side by side may well be the same courses in many instances. Foreign language or other research tool requirements will be truly functional. A comprehensive examination which is typically broader and less specialized than the usual Ph.D. comprehensive examination but not less demanding will be required upon the completion of formal course work.

Second, prospective college teachers will take an appropriate amount of formal course work and seminars in such areas as the psychology of learning, the history and sociology of higher education, and the responsibilities of faculty members within an institutional setting.

Third, as a parallel to the traditional research training for the Ph.D. degree, a structured teaching or other appropriate internship will be required. This normally will not be met by the usual teaching assistantships. The teaching internship will include progressive and responsible classroom experience in regular courses, preferably in more than one kind of course. The internship will normally be held for one year and it will be supervised, criticized, and evaluated by experienced faculty members and reinforced by relevant course work in teaching methods which are applicable to the student's particular discipline.

Fourth, the development of the capacity and habit of reading, understanding, and interpreting the results of new research and pedagogical developments appearing in the literature of the field will be encouraged.

Fifth, development of the student's ability to apply new, significant disciplinary research and teaching techniques for the benefit of college teaching is a significant part of the student's graduate education for the Doctor of Arts degree.

Sixth, independent investigation of an area in the subject matter field will lead to a suitable written thesis. Such an investigation might take the form of research on teaching problems and may make a contribution to the teaching of the subject matter. The evaluation and synthesis of materials that are potentially valuable in college teaching but have not yet been reviewed may also be acceptable.

Appendix C: Sandwich Programs in Great Britain and Cooperative Education Programs in the United States

TECHNICAL TRAINING IN ENGLAND

Several English technical education programs employ alternating periods of training at work and full-time college study. The major patterns for this type of training are:

a two-day release, or two days per week instead of one;

b "block" release, in which the aggregate of full-time periods at college, over the whole course, averages eighteen weeks per year or less (such as, for example, one full term of twelve or thirteen weeks per year, or one week in every three);

c "sandwich" or "thin-sandwich" release, in which the full-time periods at work and at college are of about six months each;

d "thick-sandwch" release, in which the full-time college periods are longer than six months (such as nine months at college and three in industry; or a year in industry, followed by a three-year course at a university, and then by another year in industry); and

e a kind which might be called "inside-out-sandwich", in which, for example, a full year in industry occupies the second or third year of an otherwise full-time four-year course.

. . . Most sandwich students are, like part-time students, "works-based", being employed as student apprentices and paid a wage by their firms whilst at college and at work. But a few are "college-based", that is to say, not regular employees at all, but eligible for grant from their authorities whilst at college and paid a wage only during the works-training parts of their courses. The latter parts are arranged by the colleges in consultation with co-operating firms. (SOURCE: A. J. Peters, *British Further Education,* Pergamon Press, Oxford, 1967.)

COOPERATIVE PROGRAMS IN THE UNITED STATES

In 1921, Antioch, a liberal arts college, included alternating work and study among its degree requirements. Today, over 60 American colleges include some type of work or service experience as an integral part of their educational programs.

In most American programs the student is college-based rather than work-based as in the English "sandwich" programs.

Recently, Chancellor Bowker of the City University of New York has proposed a university B.A. degree program that consists of three years on campus and one year of off-campus experience selected jointly by the student and faculty committee to contribute to the student's educational growth and development. Under the proposal, the off-campus year may include, but not be limited to, independent study or research, foreign travel, work experiences, artistic or other creative endeavors, community action or civic service, or any other activities deemed academically appropriate and educationally sound by the student and faculty.

Appendix D: College-Level Examination Program

The College Entrance Examination Board states that the purpose of its College-Level Examination Program is to "enable individuals who have acquired their education in nontraditional ways to demonstrate their academic achievement." The program was begun in 1965 with financial aid from the Carnegie Corporation. By the fall of 1969, nearly 400 colleges stated they would give credit through the program, although policies on amount of credit available and minimum acceptable scores varied among the colleges. Tests may be taken at any of the 59 CLEP test centers in the larger urban areas of the United States or by enrolled students at many universities. Wide use of the program is also made in the armed forces. About 1 million tests have been administered under this program. Tests are now given in more than 20 subjects with tests in several additional subjects being developed.

Appendix E: Bachelor's Degree in Liberal Studies, University of Oklahoma

In 1961, the University of Oklahoma established a program leading to the degree of Bachelor of Liberal Studies. In 1968 this program was expanded to include a Master of Liberal Studies. This program makes it possible for a student to obtain a degree largely through directed independent study. He is required to participate in four short-term residential seminars (three that are three weeks in length and one which is four weeks in length) during the course of his study. For each of the four major areas of study he receives basic reading lists and other advice concerning independent study as needed.

COLLEGE CREDIT FOR NONRESIDENT WORK Several other American institutions, such as Syracuse University, Goddard College, and the University of South Florida, have programs similar to the University of Oklahoma program. Recently, Ewald T. Nyquist, the New York State commissioner of education, announced that he would establish an "external degree" program to enable qualified persons not enrolled in college to earn degrees through independent study and examinations.

Some universities and colleges now permit a portion of the required credits for a degree to be earned through correspondence work in courses offered through TV or radio, or by examination through the College-Level Examination Program.

Appendix F: Total Registered and Elapsed Time from B.A. to Ph.D. by Field (1964-1966) Doctorates

Field	Total registered time		Total elapsed time	
	(Median)	(Mode)	(Median)	(Mode)
Physical sciences and engineering	5.1	5	6.3	5
Biological sciences	5.3	5	7.3	5
Social sciences	5.3	5	8.0	5
Art and humanities	5.7	5	9.5	6
Professional fields	6.0	4	10.8	7
Education	6.8	5	13.8	15

SOURCE: *Doctoral Recipients from United States Universities, 1958–1966*, National Academy of Sciences, Publication 1489, Washington, D.C., 1967.

Carnegie Commission on Higher Education
Publications in Print

LESS TIME, MORE OPTIONS:
EDUCATION BEYOND THE HIGH SCHOOL
a special report and recommendations by the Commission

BRIDGES TO UNDERSTANDING:
INTERNATIONAL PROGRAMS OF AMERICAN COLLEGES AND UNIVERSITIES
Irwin T. Sanders and Jennifer C. Ward

HIGHER EDUCATION AND THE NATION'S HEALTH:
POLICIES FOR MEDICAL AND DENTAL EDUCATION
a special report and recommendations by the Commission

GRADUATE AND PROFESSIONAL EDUCATION, 1980:
A SURVEY OF INSTITUTIONAL PLANS
Lewis B. Mayhew

THE AMERICAN COLLEGE AND AMERICAN CULTURE:
SOCIALIZATION AS A FUNCTION OF HIGHER EDUCATION
Oscar and Mary F. Handlin

RECENT ALUMNI AND HIGHER EDUCATION:
A SURVEY OF COLLEGE GRADUATES
Joe L. Spaeth and Andrew M. Greeley

CHANGE IN EDUCATIONAL POLICY:
SELF-STUDIES IN SELECTED COLLEGES AND UNIVERSITIES
Dwight R. Ladd

THE OPEN-DOOR COLLEGES:
POLICIES FOR COMMUNITY COLLEGES
a special report and recommendations by the Commission

QUALITY AND EQUALITY: REVISED RECOMMENDATIONS
NEW LEVELS OF FEDERAL RESPONSIBILITY FOR HIGHER EDUCATION
a supplement to the 1968 special report by the Commission

STATE OFFICIALS AND HIGHER EDUCATION:
A SURVEY OF THE OPINIONS AND EXPECTATIONS OF POLICY MAKERS IN NINE STATES
Heinz Eulau and Harold Quinley

A CHANCE TO LEARN:
AN ACTION AGENDA FOR EQUAL OPPORTUNITY IN HIGHER EDUCATION
a special report and recommendations by the Commission

ACADEMIC DEGREE STRUCTURES:
INNOVATIVE APPROACHES
PRINCIPLES OF REFORM IN DEGREE STRUCTURES IN THE UNITED STATES
Stephen H. Spurr

COLLEGES OF THE FORGOTTEN AMERICANS:
A PROFILE OF STATE COLLEGES AND REGIONAL UNIVERSITIES
E. Alden Dunham

FROM BACKWATER TO MAINSTREAM:
A PROFILE OF CATHOLIC HIGHER EDUCATION
Andrew M. Greeley

ALTERNATIVE METHODS OF FEDERAL FUNDING FOR HIGHER EDUCATION
Ron Wolk

INVENTORY OF CURRENT RESEARCH ON HIGHER EDUCATION 1968
Dale M. Heckman and Warren Bryan Martin

QUALITY AND EQUALITY:
NEW LEVELS OF FEDERAL RESPONSIBILITY
FOR HIGHER EDUCATION
*a special report and recommendations by the
Commission, with 1970 revisions*

*The following reprints are available from the Carnegie Commission on
Higher Education, 1947 Center Street, Berkeley, California 94704*

RESOURCES FOR HIGHER EDUCATION:
AN ECONOMIST'S VIEW
Theodore W. Schultz

STUDENT PROTEST—
AN INSTITUTIONAL AND NATIONAL PROFILE
Harold L. Hodgkinson

INDUSTRIAL RELATIONS AND UNIVERSITY
RELATIONS
Clark Kerr

WHAT'S BUGGING THE STUDENTS?
Kenneth Keniston